The Sayings of Sir Walter Scott

Sayings of Jane Austen
Sayings of Lord Byron
Sayings of Winston Churchill
Sayings of Charles Dickens
Sayings of Disraeli
Sayings of F. Scott Fitzgerald
Sayings of Benjamin Franklin
Sayings of Dr Johnson
Sayings of James Joyce
Sayings of John Keats
Sayings of Rudyard Kipling
Sayings of D.H. Lawrence
Sayings of Somerset Maugham
Sayings of Nietzsche
Sayings of George Orwell
Sayings of Dorothy Parker
Sayings of Ezra Pound
Sayings of Sir Walter Scott
Sayings of Shakespeare
Sayings of Bernard Shaw
Sayings of Sydney Smith
Sayings of R.L. Stevenson
Sayings of Jonathan Swift
Sayings of Leo Tolstoy
Sayings of Anthony Trollope
Sayings of Mark Twain
Sayings of Oscar Wilde
Sayings of W.B. Yeats
Sayings of the Bible
Sayings of the Buddha
Sayings of Jesus
Sayings of Moses
Sayings of Muhammad

The Sayings of

SIR WALTER
SCOTT

edited by
Eric Anderson

DUCKWORTH

For Patricia and Jean

First published in 1995 by
Gerald Duckworth & Co. Ltd.
The Old Piano Factory
48 Hoxton Square, London N1 6PB
Tel: 0171 729 5986
Fax: 0171 729 0015

Introduction and editorial arrangement
© 1995 by Eric Anderson

A catalogue record for this book is available
from the British Library

ISBN 0 7156 2680 9

Typeset by Ray Davies
Printed in Great Britain by
Redwood Books Ltd, Trowbridge

Contents

7   Introduction

13 Scotland & the Scots

16 England & the English

18 Ireland & the Irish

19 Foreigners & Travel

23 Great Contemporaries & Literary Giants

27 Education

30 Women, Love & Marriage

32 Money

33 Law & Lawyers

34 Music

36 Religion

39 Stoicism & Self-help

40 Solitude, Society & Politics

43 Old Age & Death

45 Authors & Publishers

48 Poetry, Novels & Other Writing

52 Scott on Himself

56 Rules for Living

59 Observations & Opinions

The last of all the Bards was he,
Who sung of Border minstrelsy.

Introduction

Walter Scott was the foremost literary figure of his day. Born in 1771, and outliving by the time of his death in 1832 all the great romantics except Coleridge and Wordsworth, he was incomparably better known than any of them. The narrative poems with which he made his name – *The Lay of the Last Minstrel*, *Marmion*, *The Lady of the Lake* and the others – earned him an offer of the poet laureateship. (He turned it down in favour of Southey on the grounds that he already held public office under the Crown as Sheriff of Selkirkshire and Clerk of Session in the Edinburgh courts.) *Waverley*, published in 1814 when he was forty-three, was an instant sensation. The Waverley Novels, as Scott's twenty-six novels came to be called, were the world's first real historical novels and the world's first best-sellers. They paved the way for the great popular novels of the Victorian age, influenced Pushkin and Tolstoy as well as George Eliot and Dickens, and earned him the money to buy land, to plant trees and to build Abbotsford in the Scottish border country near Melrose. They were translated into almost every European language, and new collected editions continued to find a ready market for a century after his death. Although only *Lucia di Lammermoor* is unfailingly popular today, Scott inspired more operas than any other writer except Shakespeare. His literary reputation introduced him to the great men of his time, and he became intimate with Wordsworth, Coleridge and Byron, Lawrence, Turner and Humphry Davy, Canning and Wellington. The Prince Regent conferred a baronetcy on him, and when he became George IV encouraged Scott to arrange for him the first modern royal visit to Scotland.

The economic depression of 1825-6 turned what had seemed a charmed life to disaster. Scott was the principal partner in the business of his old schoolfellow James Ballantyne who printed his novels and, by a system of double proofs, helped him to preserve his anonymity. (The novels were ostensibly the work of 'The Author of Waverley' or transmitted by 'Jedediah Cleishbotham'.) Ballantyne did much business with Constable, the most flamboyant of the several publishers who had been responsible for Scott's works. In January 1826 the London firm of Hurst and Robinson went bankrupt and called in the debts owing to them. That brought Constable down, and with him Ballantyne. As limited liability had not yet been introduced, Scott, as Ballantyne's partner, found himself responsible for all Ballantyne's debts, and (because Ballantyne and Constable had been supporting each other with loans) for much of Constable's debt as well. He could have declared himself bankrupt. Indeed that was the course he would have recommended, he said, to a legal client. Had he done so he would have paid off about one sixth of the whole sum of nearly £130,000 and been free to re-establish himself as a lawyer and an author. But for that line of action, he would, as he put it, in a Court of Honour deserve to lose his spurs. Furthermore he had, without the slightest inkling of the crisis ahead, only a few months before removed Abbotsford and its estate from the reach of his creditors by settling them on his eldest son on his marriage to a young heiress. Malicious tongues would protest that he had foreseen the collapse in his fortunes and acted to avoid the consequences. So he refused the easy route of bankruptcy and instead persuaded his creditors to allow him to write on their behalf until the debt was paid off. 'This right hand shall do it', he promised himself in his *Journal*, and that promise was kept.

For the last six years of his life – years during which he lost his wife and his only grandson, and suffered from depression and the ills of increasing age – he wrote, day in and day out, weekdays and Sundays, to pay off the mountain of debt. It is a popular but erroneous belief that the bulk of the Waverley Novels were written for this purpose. In fact twenty-one novels, including most of those that are best-known, had already been written. Only five novels belong to the sad final years. His longest work during this time was a nine-volume *Life of Napoleon* and the most successful the first collected edition of his novels, to which he contributed new introductions and notes. It was this 'Magnum Opus', as he called it, which in the end liquidated the debt.

Not, however, before Scott's death. In the summer of 1832, worn out and after suffering several strokes, Scott returned from Naples, where he had gone in a vain effort to recover his health. He died at his beloved Abbotsford on 21 September. Constable's son-in-law Cadell, who was by then Scott's publisher, took over the debt from the family in return for the copyrights in the novels – a bargain which pleased the family at the time and which ultimately made a fortune for the sharp young publisher.

'No sounder piece of British manhood was put together in that eighteenth century of Time', was Thomas Carlyle's verdict on his fellow-countryman. It is hard to think that anyone who knew Scott would have dissented. He was as fine a man as he was writer.

Since the Waverley Novels were originally published anonymously, the author was often referred to as 'The Great Unknown'. In the later twentieth century the Great Unknown has become the Great Unread. University students assess nineteenth-century fiction without feeling the need to read the father of the nineteenth-century novel; the general reader prefers something shorter and more modern. Those who assume that a novelist who is not much read must therefore be unreadable will find these *Sayings* a pleasant surprise. There is wit as well as wisdom, and they reveal a man of immense common-sense with clear, forceful and often astonishingly modern views. Only on two topics are his opinions likely to grate on modern ears. If he is severe on the French he is, we should realise, reflecting the feelings of almost everybody who lived through the years when world affairs were dominated by the towering and baneful figure of Bonaparte. His strictures on Catholicism were a reflection of his upbringing in presbyterian Edinburgh, reinforced by what he saw among the poor in Ireland in 1825. In the end, however, he became a supporter of Catholic emancipation.

Assembling the sayings in this book led me to an interesting realisation about Scott's style. It is almost as if there were in reality two Scotts, the 'Author of Waverley' who wrote novels, and the Walter Scott who dashed off letters to friends. In the novels the good sayings are few and far between and usually wordily expressed. In letters to family and friends, and in the journal he kept for the last six years of his life, he is often entertaining, indiscreet and master of a telling turn of phrase. The explanation may be that there were indeed two different *personae* at work. Although many speculated correctly that Scott must be the Great Unknown, he did not admit it until after his financial ruin. He was conscious therefore of the need to preserve his anonymity and concerned to distance 'The Author of Waverley' and 'Jedediah Cleishbotham' from the Walter Scott of Abbotsford and Edinburgh who joked with his fellow-lawyers and country neighbours and told dinner-table stories about Scottish characters and

Scottish history. The rather formal style of the novels, written under these pseudonyms, seems to have been the result.

In this respect his printer, James Ballantyne, did not help. It was he who corrected Scott's text and, to modern taste, over-punctuated it. By contrast Scott's letters, of which he wrote thousands, were hurried off spontaneously and speak with the authentic voice of the real man. His *Journal*, too, a courageous, painful record of the heroic years after his financial crash, is unpremeditated and natural.

Inevitably, therefore, this little collection relies more heavily on Scott's personal writings than on his novels. Sometimes the same sentiments occur in both, and when that happens I have tried to choose those that are more pithily or more entertainingly expressed. But from whatever source they come these are clearly the sayings of an admirable man and a very considerable writer. The continuing neglect of his novels is puzzling. A revival of interest is long overdue.

Sources and abbreviations

Letters refers to the twelve-volume *Letters of Sir Walter Scott*, ed. H.J.C. Grierson and others, Constable, 1932-7.

Journal refers to *The Journal of Sir Walter Scott*, ed. W.E.K. Anderson, Clarendon Press, 1972.

Life refers to the ten-volume *Life of Sir Walter Scott*, J.G. Lockhart, Cadell, 1838.

In a few places spelling has been regularised (for instance where Scott used 'd' rather than 'ed' in the perfect tense), words omitted in error have been silently inserted and some light punctuation added to a few quotations from Scott's *Letters* and *Journal*.

Scotland & the Scots

Breathes there the man, with soul so dead,
Who never to himself hath said,
This is my own, my native land!
Whose heart hath ne'er within him burn'd,
As home his footsteps he hath turn'd
From wandering on a foreign strand!

O Caledonia! stern and wild,
Meet nurse for a poetic child!
Land of brown heath and shaggy wood,
Land of the mountain and the flood,
Land of my sires! what mortal hand
Can e'er untie the filial band
That knits me to thy rugged strand!

Lay of the Last Minstrel, canto 6

[On Edinburgh]
Such dusky grandeur clothed the height,
Where the huge Castle holds its state,
And all the steep slope down,
Whose ridgy back heaves to the sky,
Piled deep and massy, close and high,
Mine own romantic town.

Marmion, canto 4

If thou wouldst view fair Melrose aright,
Go visit it by the pale moonlight;
For the gay beams of lightsome day
Gild, but to flout, the ruins grey.

Lay of the Last Minstrel, canto 2

Perthshire forms the fairest portion of the northern
kingdom.

Fair Maid of Perth, ch. 1

His countenance was of the true Scottish cast, strongly marked, and rather harsh in features, with a shrewd and penetrating eye, and a countenance in which habitual gravity was enlivened by a cast of ironical humour.

Antiquary, ch. 1

As far as I have observed no two nations in Europe resemble each other less than the English and Scotch – I mean the middle classes for those of the highest ranks by travel and company soon rub off all marks of Nationality. The Englishman is very apt to partake of the feelings of those around him and nowhere is a popular impulse so univerally acknowledged. Now my Countrymen are sly restive and contradictory in their dispositions and I sincerely believe that utter starvation will hardly bring twelve of them to unite in one verdict unless their national pride is concerned in the question in which cause an hundred will have but one voice.

Letters, II.133

In Scotland men of all ranks but especially the middling and the lower classes are linked together by ties which give them a strong interest in each others' success in life and it is amazing the exertion which men will make to support and assist persons with whom you would suppose them connected by very remote ties of consanguinity and by no other link whatever.

Ibid., IV.456

Assuredly Heaven did not form the Caledonian for the gay world; and his efforts at ease, grace, and gaiety resemble only the clumsy gambols of the ass in the fable.

St. Ronan's Well, ch. 19

The Scotch are a cautious people.

Guy Mannering, ch. 55

The Scotch are not a people who speedily admit innovation, even when it comes in the shape of improvement.

Rob Roy, ch. 30

Scottish audiences … are certainly not inclined to give applause upon credit.

Journal, 601

In giving an account of a Highlander, his pedigree is first to be considered.

Rob Roy, Introduction

There are few nations, by the way, who can boast of so much natural politeness as the Highlanders.

Waverley, ch. 29

A tincture of Jacobitism … though rather an Instinct than a principle adopted from reason forms a frequent feature in the character of the animal called a thorough bred Scotsman.

Letters, XII.197

If a man relaxed the custom of his exercise in Scotland for a bad day he is not like to resume it in a hurry.

Journal, 521

Frank Osbaldistone: 'Fine weather for your work, my friend.'
Andrew Fairservice: 'It's no that muckle to be compleened o'.'

Rob Roy, ch. 6

The mail-coach and the Berwick smacks have done more than the Union in altering our national character, sometimes for the better and sometimes for the worse.

Letters, I. 285

London licks the butter off our bread by opening a better market for ambition. Were it not for the difference of the religion and laws poor Scotland could hardly keep a man that is worth having.

Journal, 538

If you *unscotch* us you will find us damned mischievous Englishmen.

Letters, IX.472

England & the English

England was merry England, when
Old Christmas brought his sports again.
'Twas Christmas broach'd the mightiest ale;
'Twas Christmas told the merriest tale;
A Christmas gambol oft could cheer
The poor man's heart through half the year.

Marmion, canto 6

One of those old-fashioned Gothic parish churches
which are frequent in England, the most cleanly, decent,
and reverential places of worship that are, perhaps,
anywhere to be found in the Christian world.

Heart of Mid-Lothian, ch. 30

The view of Oxford from the Maudlin Bridge which I
used to think one of the most beautiful in the world.

Journal, 243

[London:] That immense hash of a city.

Ibid., 474

… a yellow fog which is the curse of London. I would
hardly take my share of it for a share of its wealth and its
curiosity, a vile double distilled fog of the most
intolerable kind.

Ibid., 662-3

But who cares for the whipped cream of London society?

Ibid., 462-3

To be acquainted with persons of mere *ton* is a nuisance
and a scrape – to be known to persons of real fashion
and fortune is in London a very great advantage.

Ibid., 36

I would like to be there were it but to see how the cat jumps. One knows nothing of the world if you are absent from it so long as I have been.   *Ibid.*, 208

A Londoner with all the acuteness, address, and audacity which belong peculiarly to the youth of a metropolis.   *Fortunes of Nigel*, ch. 1

Well mannered and sensible are the Southern boys. I suppose the sun brings them forwards.
          Journal, 298

English boys have this advantage that they are well bred and can converse when ours are regular-built cubs – I am not sure if it is an advantage in the long run. It is a temptation to premature display.   *Ibid.*, 272

In general the English understand conversation well. There is that ready deference for the claims of every one who wishes to speak time about.   *Ibid.*, 469

The art of quiet and entertaining conversation which is always easy as well as entertaining is I think chiefly known in England. In Scotland we are pedantic and wrangle or we run away with the harrows on some topic we chance to be discursive upon.
          Ibid., 191

My countrymen, taken in their general capacity, are not people to have recourse to in adverse circumstances. John Bull is a better beast in misfortune.
          Letters, X.410

Every Englishman has a tolerably accurate sense of law and justice.   *The Two Drovers*, ch. 2

That dogged spirit of courage so peculiar to the English.
          Betrothed, ch. 27

The Englishman's characteristic of More Money than wit.
          Journal, 703

Ireland & the Irish

The inhabitants, from the peer to the peasant, are certainly the kindest people in the world.

Letters, IX.263

I do not think even our Scottish hospitality can match that of Ireland.

Ibid., IX.195

They are certainly a very odd people and but for that ugly humour of murdering which is in full decline they would be the most amusing and easy to live with in the world.

Ibid., IX.211

While a Scotchman is thinking about the term day, or if easy on that subject about Hell in the next world, while an Englishman is making a little hell of his own in the present because his muffin is not well roasted, Pat's mind is always turned to fun and ridicule. They are terribly excitable to be sure and will murther you on slight suspicion and find out next day that it was all a mistake and that it was not yourself they meant to kill at all at all.

Journal, 3

The protestants of the old school or determined Orangemen are a very fine race but dangerous for the quiet of a country.

Letters, IX.239

I do not believe either party care a bit for what is called emancipation only that the Catholics desire it because the protestants are not willing they should have it and the protestants desire to withold it because the want of it mortifies the Catholic.

Ibid., IX.239-40

I am much honoured by the good opinion of the Irish nation whose praise must be always most valuable to a poet because they are not only a people of infinite genius but of a warmth of heart and feeling not perhaps generally appreciated either by your countrymen or mine.

Ibid., II.384

Foreigners & Travel

Those who wish to see me should be able to speak my language.

Journal, 492

Talking of Abbotsford it begins to be haunted by too much company of every kind. But especially foreigners. I do not like them. I hate fine waistcoats and breast pins upon dirty shirts.

Ibid., 10

I make it a rule seldom to read and never to answer foreign letters from literary folks. It leads to nothing but the battledore and shuttlecock intercourse of compliments as light as cork and feathers.

Ibid., 278

I am truly glad you are going abroad – nothing gives such a fillip to the imagination.

Letters, IV.263

To see foreign parts gives I think more the feelings of youth to those of an advanced age than anything they can engage in.

Ibid., IV.306

The Americans are so like to the British, the British to the Americans, that they have not much patience with each other for not being in all respects the same with each other.

Ibid., XI.353

I see dissensions between us and the Americans as threatening infinite disadvantage to both Nations and offering no adequate advantage to either.

Ibid., XI.356

[The Americans] are a people possessed of very considerable energy quickened and brought into eager action by an honourable love of their country and pride in their institutions but they are as yet rude in their ideas of social intercourse, and totally ignorant speaking generally of all the art of good breeding which consists chiefly in a postponement of one's own petty wishes or comforts to those of others. By rude questions, free and unfeeling observations, an absolute disrespect to other people's feelings and a ready indulgence of their own they make one feverish in their company though perhaps you may be ashamed to confess the reason. But this will wear off and is wearing away.

Ibid., VIII.188-9

There are no braver men than the Germans.

Talisman, ch. 11

A more inefficient yet a more resolved class of men than the Spaniards were never conceived.

Journal, 648

Paris I am not anxious to see again but I trust you will see it once. There is more of good and bad in it than anywhere else in the world. I do not mean *moral* good of which there is rather a paucity but worldly grandeur and display.

Letters, IV.263

Of all capitals, that of France affords most numerous objects of curiosity, accessible in the easiest manner; and it may be therefore safely pronounced one of the most entertaining places of residence which can be chosen by an idle man.

Paul's Letters to his Kinsfolk, 288

[French flattery:] One can swallow a great deal of whipped cream to be sure and it does not hurt an old stomach.
    [*One day later*] I wish for a little of the old Scotch causticity. I am something like the bee that sips treacle.

Journal, 231-2

Ere I leave *la belle France* however it is fit I should
express my gratitude for the unwontedly kind reception
which I met with at all hands. It would be an unworthy
piece of affectation did I not allow that I have been
pleased – highly pleased – to find a species of literature
intended only for my own country has met such an
extensive and favourable reception in a foreign land
where there was so much *a priori* to oppose its progress,
Ibid., 235

The French language is certainly the most unfit for
Poetry that ever was uttered. I do not believe there are
twenty words in the language that can be properly
termed *poetical*, that is that are not equally used in Poetry
or Prose, and this alone gives poverty and meanness to
their verses.
Letters, III.524

Are not you sensible of the difference between language
and language when turning from even the best French
Poets to the richness of the Italians? The difference in
their music or in their painting is scarce more
remarkable – it is positive repose and enjoyment – there
is something hard and meagre and cold and affected in
the French diction.
Ibid., III.531

It is mortifying that Dante seemed to think nobody
worth being sent to hell but his own Italians, whereas
other people had every bit as great rogues in their
families, whose misdeeds were suffered to pass with
impunity.   *Life*, X.187

Much struck with the beauty of the Bay of Naples. It is
insisted that my arrival has been a signal for the greatest
eruption from Vesuvius which that mountain has
favoured us with for many a day. I can only say as the
Frenchman said of the comet supposed to foretell his
own death, 'Ah, Messieurs, la Comète me fait trop
d'honneur.'
Journal, 691

Methinks I will not die quite happy without having seen something of that Rome of which I have read so much.

Letters, IV.477

[The Tyrolese:] I cannot but think their *udalling*, if this be the word, is a variation or set of variations upon the tones of a Jack ass.

Journal, 594

The increasing powers of Steam which like you I look on 'half proud half sad half angry and half pleased' in doing so much for the commercial world promise something also for the sociable, and like Prince Hossein's tapestry will I think one day waft friends together in the course of a few hours and for aught we may be able to tell bring Hampstead and Abbotsford within the distance of 'will you dine with us quietly to-morrow'.

Letters, VIII.56-7

Who knows how soon time and space may be actually abolished and Abbotsford be as near St. Paul's as White Chapel.

Ibid., X.284

Great Contemporaries &
Literary Giants

What a miserable thing it is that our royal family cannot be quiet and decent at least if not correct and moral in their deportment. Old farmer George's manly simplicity, modesty of expense and domestic virtue saved this country at its most perilous crisis for it is inconceivable the number of persons whom these qualities united in his behalf who would have felt but coldly the abstract duty of supporting a crown less worthily worn.

Letters, III.478

The excellent private character of the Old King [*George III*] gave him great advantages as the Head of a free government. I fear the [New King] will long experience the inconveniences of not having attended to his own.

Ibid., III.100-1

[George IV] converses with so much ease and elegance that you lose thoughts of the prince in admiring the well-bred and accomplished gentleman. He is in many respects the model of a British monarch.

Journal, 218

I was presented to the little Princess Victoria, I hope they will change her name, the heir apparent to the crown as things now stand ... She is fair like the royal family but does not look as if she would be pretty.

Ibid., 478

There will be no permanent peace in Europe till Buonaparte sleeps with the tyrants of old.

Letters, III.381

[Napoleon] might have been a great man and was only a great soldier – he might have been the benefactor of the human race and he was the cause of more blood being spilled than had flowed for an hundred years before. He lowered the standard of virtue and public feeling among the French and soiled their soldierly character by associating it with perfidy and dishonour.

Ibid., VIII.264-5

In fact my trust is and has long been in that one man [Wellington] who possesses in a higher degree the gift of common sense than in anyone I have heard or read of. He is the only Man of whom I could say like Robert Bruce to the Lord of the Isles 'My trust is constant in thee'.

Ibid., XI.141

I had to-day a most kind and friendly letter from the Duke of Wellington, which is a thing to be vain of. He is a wonderful man to have climbed to such a height without ever slipping his foot. Who would have said in 1815 that the Duke would stand still higher in 1829? And yet it indubitably is so.

Journal, 566

What is become of William Pitt? It is astonishing how the loss of one man has deranged the wisdom and disorganized the force of this mighty people.

Letters, II.336

The blockheads talk of my being like Shakespeare – not fit to tie his brogues.

Journal, 252

The Commentators of Shakespeare have overburthened the text with notes and with disputes trivial in themselves and not always conducted either with taste or temper.

Letters, XII.450

A hasty recollection will convince any of us how much better we are acquainted with those parts of English history which that immortal bard has dramatized than with any other portion of British story.

Peveril of the Peak, Prefatory Letter

[Holy Trinity Church, Stratford:] What a magic does the locality possess. There are stately monuments of forgotten families but when you have seen Shakespeare what care we for the rest?   *Journal*, 454

Goethe, an author born to arouse the slumbering fame of his country.   *Anne of Geierstein*, ch. 17

Goethe is different and a wonderful fellow, the Ariosto at once, and almost the Voltaire of Germany.
     Journal, 278

Johnson's rudeness possibly arose from his retaining till late in life the habits of a pedagogue, who is a man among boys and a boy among men, and having the bad taste to think it more striking to leap over the little differences and courtesies which form the turnpike gates in society, and which fly open on payment of a trifling tribute.   *Letters*, XI.115

[Boswell] was always labouring at notoriety, and, having failed in attracting it in his own person, he hooked his little bark to them whom he thought most likely to leave harbour, and so shone with reflected light, like the rat that eat the malt that lay in the house that Jack built.
     Ibid., XI.117

Long life to thy fame and peace to thy soul, Rob Burns. When I want to express a sentiment which I feel strongly, I find the phrase in Shakespeare or thee.
     Journal, 252

I saw that distinguished poet only once and that many years since ... But Burns was so remarkable a man that his features remain impressed on my mind as I had seen him only yesterday.   *Letters*, XI.264-5

[Burns:] I once dined in company with him, and remember well the flash of his dark brown eye. I think his pictures are not like him.   *Ibid.*, IX.280

I think it a curious point of Burns' character ... that he copied over the very same letters or great part of them and sent them to different individuals.   *Ibid.*, X.456

I felt the prudence of giving way [as a poet] before the more forcible and powerful genius of Byron.

Ibid., VI.506

[Byron:] A man of real goodness of heart, and the kindest and best feelings, miserably thrown away by his foolish contempt of public opinion. *Life,* VII.323

[Byron:] What a pity that a man of such exquisite genius will not be contented to be happy on the ordinary terms! I declare my heart bleeds when I think of him, self-banished from the country to which he is an honour.

Letters, IV.319

That eccentric but admirable poet, Coleridge.

Ibid., I.146

Wordsworth in particular is such a character as only exists in romance – virtuous, simple, and unaffectedly restricting every want and wish to the bounds of a very narrow income in order to enjoy the literary and poetical leisure which his happiness consists in. *Ibid.,* I.287

Wordsworth is a man and a gentleman every inch of him unless when he is mounted on his critical hobby horse and tells one Pope is no poet. He might as well say Wellington is no soldier because he wears a blue great coat and not a coat of burnished mail.

Ibid., VIII.307

I do not at all acquiesce in his system of poetry and I think he has injured his own fame by adhering to it. But a better or more sensible man I do not know than W.W.

Journal, 474

Landseer's dogs were the most magnificent things I ever saw, leaping and bounding and grinning on the canvas.

Ibid., 88

Read again and for the third time at least Miss Austen's very finely written novel of *Pride and Prejudice.* That young lady had a talent for describing the involvements and feelings and characters of ordinary life which is to me the most wonderful I ever met with. *Ibid.,* 114

Education

A schoolmaster has almost always something pedantic about him, from being long and constantly a man among boys.   *Letters, VIII.214*

Many a clever boy is flogged into a dunce and many an original composition corrected into mediocrity.
Journal, 164

I am an enemy to corporal punishment. But there are many boys who will not attend without it. It is an instant and irresistible motive, and I love boys' heads too much to spoil them at the expense of their opposite extremity.
Ibid., 252

I am more and more convinced of the excellence of the English monastic institutions of Cambridge and Oxford. They cannot do all that may be expected but there is at least the exclusion of many temptations to dissipation of mind. Whereas with us, supposing a young man to have any pretensions to keep good society ... he is almost pulled to pieces by speculating mamas and flirting misses. If a man is poor, plain, and indifferently connected, he may have excellent oportunities of study at Edinburgh; otherwise he should beware of it.
Letters, VIII.256

[Colleges:] When their attentions are to be given to the departments of the cook and the butler all zeal in the nobler paths of education is apt to decay.
Journal, 497

[A boy at Eton:] The talents, good sense and knowledge of the world, picked up at one of the great English schools (and it is one of their most important results) will prevent him from being deceived.   *Ibid., 188*

I have guarded against nothing more in the education of my own family, than against their acquiring habits of self-willed caprice and domination.

Life, I.35-6

Habits of firm and assiduous application, of gaining the art of controlling, directing and concentrating the powers of his mind for earnest investigation [is] an art far more essential than even that intimate acquaintance with classical learning, which is the primary object of study.   *Waverley*, ch. 3

The commencement of every profession is necessarily dull and disagreeable to youths of lively genius.

Letters, VII.7

The study of grammar from its very asperities is calculated to teach youth that patient labour which is necessary to the useful exertion of the understanding upon every other branch of knowledge.

Ibid., VI.293-4

The purpose [of Constable's *Miscellany*] is to bring all the standard works both in sciences and the liberal arts within the reach of the lower classes and enable them thus to use with advantage the education which is given them at every hand. To make boys learn to read and then place no good books within their reach is to give men an appetite and leave nothing in the pantry save unwholesome and poisonous food which, depend upon it, they will eat rather than starve.

Journal, 28

The best of luxuries, the luxury of knowledge.

Guy Mannering, ch. 24

Boys are uncommonly just in their feelings, and at least equally generous.   *Life*, I.40

Promises made to young folks should always be solemnly observed.   *Letters*, VI.180

To give education to dull mediocrity is a flinging of the children's bread to dogs – it is sharpening a hatchet on a razor-strop, which renders the strop useless and does no good to the hatchet.

Journal, 203

I have never remarked anyone, be he soldier or divine or lawyer, that was exclusively attached to the narrow habits of his own profession, but what such person became a great twaddle in good society, besides, what is of much more importance, becoming narrow-minded and ignorant of all general information.

Letters, VI.443

Men like Watt whose genius tends strongly to invent and execute those wonderful combinations which extend in such an incalculable degree the human force and command over the physical world do not come within ordinary rules.

Ibid., IX.238

I have heard higher sentiments from the lips of poor *uneducated* men and women, when exerting the spirit of severe yet gentle heroism under difficulties and afflictions, or speaking their simple thoughts as to circumstances in the lot of friends and neighbours, than I ever yet met with out of the pages of the Bible.

Life, VIII.28

Women, Love & Marriage

O, Woman! in our hours of ease,
Uncertain, coy, and hard to please,
And variable as the shade
By the light quivering aspen made;
When pain and anguish wring the brow,
A ministering angel thou!   *Marmion*, canto 6

[I hate having] to deal with ladies when they are in an
unreasonable humour.   *Journal*, 21

Women it is said go mad much seldomer than men.
                    Ibid., 205

What there is in our partiality to female beauty that
commands a species of temperate homage from the aged
as well as ecstatic admiration from the young I cannot
conceive but it is certain that a very large proportion of
some other amiable quality is too little to counterbalance
the absolute want of this advantage. I to whom beauty is
and shall henceforward be a picture still look upon it
with the quiet devotion of an old worshipper.
                    Ibid., 487

[Lady Exeter] is a beauty after my own heart – a great
deal of liveliness in the face – an absence alike of form
and of affected ease and really courteous after a genuine
and ladylike fashion.   *Ibid.*, 213

Fair, fat, and forty.   *St. Ronan's Well*, ch. 7

Where shall the lover rest,
Whom the fates sever
From his true maiden's breast,
Parted for ever?

                    Marmion, canto 3

The truth is, perhaps, the lover's pleasure, like that of the hunter, is in the chase; and that the brightest beauty loses half its merit, as the fairest flower its perfume, when the willing hand can reach it too easily.

Redgauntlet, ch. 17

Woman's faith, and woman's trust –
Write the characters in dust.

The Betrothed, ch. 20

Scarce one person out of twenty marries his first love, and scarce one out of twenty of the remainder has cause to rejoice at having done so.

Letters, VI. 208

The happiest marriages I have seen have been those which began under circumstances which required oeconomy.

Ibid., IV.24

Ladies whose husbands love foxhunting are in a poor way ... They manage the matter otherwise in France where Ladies are the Lords of the Ascendant.

Journal, 534

Only in gentle opposition like a well drilled spouse.

Ibid., 676

My new daughter-in-law seems quite alert at everything but talking much. A good listener is no bad thing however, and she always laughs in the right place.

Letters, IX.194

I do believe your destitute widow, especially if she hath a charge of children and one or two fit for patronage, is one of the most impudent animals living.

Journal, 120

Money

Avarice seldom sleeps sound.

Fortunes of Nigel, ch. 22

He who always speaks about wealth is seldom a rich man at bottom. *Surgeon's Daughter*, ch. 5

It is saving not getting that is the mother of Richess.

Journal, 550

A banker writes, only touching the needful.

Fortunes of Nigel, ch. 27

Our time is like our money. When we change a guinea the shillings escape as things of small account. When we break a day by idleness in the morning the rest of the hours lose their importance in our eye. *Journal*, 174

Capital and talent will do excellent things together; but depend on it, talent without capital will no more carry on an extensive and progressive undertaking ... than a racehorse will draw a Newcastle waggon.

Letters, IX.55

The rich much to their honour do not in general require to be so much stimulated to benevolence as to be directed in the most useful way to exert it.

Ibid., IV.448

The mere scarcity of money (so that actual wants are provided) is not poverty. It is the bitter draught to owe money which we cannot pay. *Journal*, 96

I have sometimes envied rich citizens but it was a mean and erroneous feeling ... Better be a poor gentleman after all. *Ibid.*, 471

Law & Lawyers

Mrs Bertram: That sounds like nonsense, my dear.
Mr Bertram: May be so, my dear; but it may be very good
law for all that.   *Guy Mannering*, ch. 9

One can easily, I am assured, get into a lawsuit – it is
only the getting out which is sometimes found
troublesome.   *Redgauntlet*, Letter 1

There is something sickening in seeing poor devils
drawn into great expense about trifles by interested
attorneys. But too cheap access to litigation has its evils
on the other hand, for the proneness of the lower class to
gratify spite and revenge in this way would be a
dreadful evil were they able to endure the expense.
                    Journal, 35

Most attorneys have been suspected, more or less justly,
of making their own fortune at the expense of their
clients.   *Life*, I.10

A barrister of extended practice if he has any talents at
all is the best companion in the world.
                    Journal, 466

The wigs against the wits for a guinea in point of
conversation.   *Ibid.*, 460

I suppose I am partial but I think the lawyers beat the
bishops and the bishops beat the wits.   *Ibid.*, 463

[Legal business] keeps one however in the career and
stream of actual life, which is a great advantage to a
literary man.   *Ibid.*, 396

[Jedburgh justice:] The criminals came in so fast that
they were fain to execute them first and afterwards try
them at leisure.

                    Letters, IV.211

Music

Where there is a natural turn this way … it is a great pity not to cultivate it. There is such a thing as singing the evil spirit out of others or oneself. In fact I think music (not cultivated to excess or made the introduction to too much idleness or, in men, conviviality) has a moral effect on the spirits and temper.

Letters, VIII.414

I do not know and cannot utter a note of music and complicated harmonies seem to me a babble of confused though pleasing sounds. Yet songs and simple melodies especially if connected with words and ideas have as much effect on me as on most people.

Journal, 4

My ear appears to me as dull as my voice is incapable of musical expression and yet I feel the utmost pleasure in any such music as I can comprehend, learned pieces always excepted.

Ibid., 335

I have an indifferent good ear for a jig, but your solos and sonatas give me the spleen.

Letters, IV.112 (adapted from Congreve's *Love for Love*, II.1)

[I miss] the airs of our native country which, imperfect as my musical ear is, make and always have made the most pleasing impression on me.

Journal, 29

I have a wretched ear myself, yet have great pleasure in some passages. This circumstance is the more provoking, as I believe no man in Britain had more songs of all kinds by heart than I could have mustered.

Letters, II.147

I do not understand or care about fine music but there is something in [Sandy Ballantyne's] violin which goes to the very heart.

Journal, 334

[*Ivanhoe* in Paris:] It was an opera and of course the story greatly mangled and the dialogue in a great part nonsense.

Ibid., 226

Walking within a short interval, and eying each other with looks in which self-importance and defiance might be traced, [the bagpipers] strutted, puffed, and plied their screaming instruments, each playing his own favourite tune with such a din, that if an Italian musician had lain buried within ten miles of them, he must have risen from the dead to run out of hearing.

Legend of Montrose, ch. 7

Religion

I believe in God who can change evil into good and I am confident that what befalls us is always ultimately for the best.

Journal, 372

I would if called upon die a martyr for the Christian religion, so completely is (in my poor opinion) its divine origin proved by its beneficial effects on the state of society.

Ibid., 399

Lord keep us from all temptation for we cannot be our own shepherd.

Ibid., 237

Where the heart is prepared for evil opportunity is seldom long wanting.

Heart of Mid-Lothian, ch. 1

The adaptation of religious motives to earthly policy is apt – among the infinite delusions of the human heart – to be a snare.

Journal, 461

If a Church possessed the vessels out of which the original reformers partake of the Eucharist it would be surely bad taste to melt them down and exchange them for more modern ... Law and Devotion must lose some of their dignity as often as they adopt new fashions.

Ibid., 567

[Ordination:] I have nothing to say against it but it is against my principles and feelings to recommend it.

Letters, X.5

[Ordination:] It is *entre nous* a sneaking line unless the adoption of it is dictated by a strong feeling of principle.

Ibid., X.28

[Converts:] I hate a fellow who begins with throwing away his own religion and then affects a prodigious respect for another.

Journal, 668

[The Jew] had upon his side the unyielding obstinacy of his nation, and that unbending resolution, with which Israelites have been frequently known to submit to the uttermost evils which power and violence can inflict upon them, rather than gratify their oppressors by granting their demands.

Ivanhoe, ch. 22

[The Methodists] have their faults and are peculiarly liable to those of hypocrisy and spiritual ambition and priest-craft. On the other hand they do infinite good, carrying religion into classes in Society where it would scarce be found to penetrate did it rely merely upon proof of its doctrines upon calm reason and upon rational argument. To these the Methodists add a powerful appeal to the feelings and passions and though I believe this is often exaggerated into absolute enthusiasm yet I consider upon the whole they do much to keep alive a sense of religion and the practice of morality necessarily connected with it.

Journal, 74

The world is in fact as silly as ever and a good competence of nonsense will always find believers. Animal magnetism, phrenology, have all had their believers and why not popery?

Ibid., 526

It is after all a helpless sort of superstition which with its saints' days and the influence of its ignorant bigotted priesthood destroys ambition and industrious exertion. It is rare to see the Catholic rise above the line he is born in.

Letters, IX.239

Where knowledge is diffused priest-craft must retreat.

Journal, 578

[Heaven:] They have a poor idea of the Deity and the rewards that are destined for the Just made perfect who can only adopt the literal sense of an eternal concert – a never-ending Birthday Ode. I rather suppose there should be understood some commission from the Highest, some duty to discharge with the applause of a satisfied conscience ... There would be, we must suppose, in these employments difficulties to be overcome and exertions to be made.

Ibid., 33

[The Bible:] He expressed a wish that I should read to him, and when I asked from what book, he said – 'Need you ask? There is but one.'

Life, X.209 (Lockhart, decribing Scott's deathbed)

Stoicism & Self-help

Of what use is philosophy, and I have always pretended to a little of a practical character, if it cannot teach us to do or suffer?

Journal, 371

Agere et pati Romanum est. Of all schools commend me to the Stoicks. We cannot indeed overcome our affections nor ought we if we could, but we can repress them within due bounds and avoid coaxing them to make fools of those who should be their masters.

Ibid., 25

God help – but rather God bless – man must help himself.

Ibid., 210

I like to see men think and bear themselves like men.

Ibid., 420

I am a tolerable Stoic but preach to myself in vain.

Ibid., 140

Do what is right come what will.

Ibid., 617

If we do not run some hazard in our attempts to do good where is the merit of them?

Ibid., 15

Strong men are usually good-humoured and active men often display the same elasticity of mind as of body.

Ibid., 21

Solitude, Society & Politics

The love of solitude increases by indulgence.

Journal, 89

If the question was eternal company without the power of retiring within yourself or solitary confinement for life I should say 'Turnkey, lock the cell'. *Ibid.,* 50

Solitude has one good thing – it disposes a man to work from which society is sure to divert him.

Letters, X.69

Misanthropy … I always consider as a kind of blasphemy of a shocking description. If God bears with the very worst of us we may surely endure each other. If thrown into society I always have and always will endeavour to bring pleasure with me, at least to shew willingness to please. But for all this 'I had rather live alone'. *Journal,* 121

A wise man … will receive information and fresh views of life even in the Society of Fools.

Ibid., 18

The chain of friendship however bright does not stand the attrition of constant close contact.

Ibid., 95

The time devoted to hospitality, especially to those whom I can reckon upon as sincere good friends, I never grudge but I like to –
   Welcome the coming speed the parting guest.

Ibid., 179

[Breakfast entertaining:] A neat custom that – and saves wine and wassail. *Ibid.,* 598

Dined at a public dinner ... An odd way of testifying
respect to publick characters by eating drinking and
roaring. *Ibid.*, 563

The presence of too many men of distinguished rank
and power always freezes the conversation. Each lamp
shews brightest when placed by itself; when too close
they neutralize each other. *Ibid.*, 240

What a strange scene if the surge of conversation could
suddenly ebb like the tide and show us the state of
people's real minds ...
   No eyes the rocks discover
   Which lurk beneath the deep.
Life could not be endured were it seen in reality.
Ibid., 44-5

The subject of foreign news and the political and
military situation of the country are themes upon which
every man thinks himself qualified to give an opinion.
Antiquary, ch. 19

I am glad for one that ministers have lost their income
tax – not that I have any particular objection to the tax
itself which with a few more equitable modifications is
perhaps as just as any or more so – but because it
afforded a tempting facility of raising money which was
scarce to be trusted to any ministers excepting when the
vital safety of the state is in danger. *Letters*, IV.213

The removing the taxes on tobacco and newspapers I
look upon as a bonus to mental and physical poison.
Ibid., XI.473

Royal magnificence can be only displayed by despotic
power. In England, were the most splendid street or
public building to be erected the matter must be
discussed in parliament or perhaps some sturdy cobbler
holds out and refuses to part with his stall and the whole
plan is disconcerted. Long may such impediments exist.
Journal, 224

Nature intended that population should be diffused over the soil in proportion to its extent. We have accumulated in huge cities and smothering manufactures the numbers which should be spread over the face of a country and what wonder that they should be corrupted?

Ibid., 430

One individual always manages his own concerns better than those of the country can be managed.

Letters, IV.447

So the Tories and Whigs may go be damned together as names that have distracted Old Scotland and torn asunder the most kindly feelings since the first day they were invented … And yet God knows I would fight in honourable contest with word or blow for my political opinions but I cannot permit that strife to 'mix its waters with my daily meal'.

Journal, 63

Your deepest pools, like your deepest politicians and philosophers, often turn out more shallow than expected.

Ibid., 186

Old Age & Death

The step of time is noiseless as it passes over an old man.
Journal, 563

Age is easily propitiated by attentions from the young.
Rob Roy, ch. 23

The greatest and wisest are flattered by the deference of
youth – so graceful and becoming in itself.   *Abbot*, ch. 18

To slacken your hold on life in any agreeable point of
connection is the sooner to reduce yourself to the
indifference and passive vegetation of old age.
Journal, 162

Nothing in life can be more ludicrous or contemptible
than an old man aping the passions of his youth.
Ibid., 487

I have often noticed that a kindly placid good humour is
the companion of longevity and I suspect frequently the
leading cause of it. Quick keen sharp observation with
the power of contrast and illustration disturbs this easy
current of thought.   *Ibid.*, 201

A man of eighty and upwards may be allowed to talk
long because in the nature of things he cannot have long
to talk.   *Ibid.*, 178

In his ninety-second year [Sir Robert Preston] has an
ample fortune, a sound understanding, not the least
decay of eyes ears or taste, is as big as two men and eats
like three. Yet … if his appearance renders old age
tolerable it does not make it desirable. But I fear when
Death comes we shall be unwilling for all that to part
with our bundle of sticks.   *Ibid.*, 599

Life is dear even to those who feel it a burden.

Heart of Mid-Lothian, ch. 19

I hate funerals – always did. There is such a mixture of mummery with real grief – the actual mourner perhaps heart broken and all the rest making solemn faces and whispering observations on the weather and public news and here and there a greedy fellow enjoying the cake and wine … This is a most unfilial tendency of mine for my father absolutely loved a funeral and as he was a man of a fine presence and looked the mourner well he was asked to every interment of distinction. He seemed to preserve the list of a whole bead roll of cousins merely for the pleasure of being at their funerals, which he was often asked to superintend and I suspect had sometimes to pay for.

Journal, 127

And come he slow, or come he fast,
It is but Death who comes at last.

Marmion, canto 2

Authors & Publishers

Fame depends on literature not on architecture. We are more eager to see a broken column of Cicero's villa than all those mighty labours of barbaric power [in different parts of India].

Journal, 523

No man of sense in any rank of life is, or ought to be, above accepting a just recompense for his time, and a reasonable share of the capital which owes its very existence to his exertions ... No man of honour, genius, or spirit, would make the mere love of gain the chief, far less the only, purpose of his labours. For myself, I am not displeased to find the game a winning one; yet, while I pleased the public, I should probably continue it merely for the pleasure of playing; for I have felt as strongly as most folks the love of composition which is perhaps the strongest of all instincts.

Fortunes of Nigel, Introductory Epistle

There is a great pleasure in sitting down to write with the consciousness that nothing will occur during the day to break the spell.

Journal, 96

A man of business, even a lawyer, does not take any advantage from literary acquirements; they are on the contrary sometimes supposed to divert him from his professional pursuits and so far the reputation of possessing them is a positive disadvantage ... To live the life of a mere author for bread is perhaps the most dreadful fate that can be encountered.

Letters, IV.466-7

Those powers which can make verses are applicable to the more useful and ordinary purposes of life.

Ibid., V.330

'I'd rather be a kitten, and cry, Mew!' than write the best poetry in the world on condition of laying aside common sense in the ordinary transactions and business of the world.

Ibid., VII.147

I have always remarked that literary people think themselves obliged to take somewhat of a constrained and affected turn in conversation, seeming to consider themselves as less a part of the company than something which the rest were come to see and wonder at.

Ibid., III.53

When I first saw that a literary profession was to be my fate I endeavoured by all efforts of stoicism to divest myself of that irritable degree of sensibility – or to speak plainly of Vanity – which makes the poetical race miserable and ridiculous.

Journal, 51

For ne'er
Was flattery lost on poet's ear:
A simple race! they waste their toil
For the vain tribute of a smile.

Lay of the Last Minstrel, canto 4

I think I make no habit of feeding on praise, and despise those whom I see greedy for it as I should an underbred fellow who after eating a cherry-tart proceeded to lick the plate. But when one is flagging, a little praise (if it can be had genuine and unadulterated by flattery which is as difficult to come by as the genuine Mountain dew) is a cordial after all.

Journal, 95

[Moore and I] have both seen the world too widely and too well not to contemn in our souls the imaginary consequence of literary people who walk with their noses in the air.

Ibid., 6

I do not incline to make what is called literary acquaintances.

Ibid., 461

I have always felt the value of having access to persons
of talent and genius to be the best part of a literary man's
prerogative.

Letters, V.420

Did any of my sons show poetical talent of which (to my
great satisfaction) there are no appearances, the first
thing I should do would be to inculcate upon him the
duty of cultivating some honourable profession and
qualifying himself to play a more respectable part in
Society than the mere poet.

Ibid., III.282

It is some consolation to reflect, that the best authors in
all countries have been the most voluminous.

Fortunes of Nigel, Introductory Epistle

Bookselling [is] the most ticklish and unsafe and
hazardous of all professions scarcely with the exception
of horse-jockeyship.

Letters, IV.462

A Bookseller publishes twenty Books in hopes of hitting
upon one good speculation as a person buys a parcel of
shares in a lottery in hopes of gaining a prize.

Ibid., I.380

They are very like farmers, who thrive best at a high
rent; and, in general, take most pains to sell a book that
has cost them money to purchase.

Ibid., I.388

I never wish to make a bargain by which the bookseller
shall not have his full share of the advantage because the
talent of writing and the power of selling books are two
very different things.

Ibid., VII.105

I make it a rule to cheat nobody but Booksellers, a race
on whom I have no mercy.

Ibid., XII.409

Poetry, Novels & Other Writing

I don't wonder, that, in dismissing all the other deities of Paganism, the Muse should have been retained by common consent; for, in sober reality, writing good verses seems to depend upon something separate from the volition of the author.   *Letters*, IV.380

I never yet began a poem upon a preconcerted story, and have often been well-advanced in composition before I had any idea how I was to end the work.

Ibid., V.447

I believe no man now alive writes more rapidly than I do (no great recommendation), but I never think of making verses till I have a sufficient stock of poetical ideas to supply them.   *Ibid.*, II.31-2

Poets are at liberty to commit Anachronisms for the sake of effect.

Ibid., XII.475

I think those hymns which do not immediately recall the warm and exalted language of the Bible are apt to be, however elegant, rather cold and flat for the purposes of devotion.   *Ibid.*, III.211

One poet should always speak for another.

Journal, 14

But no one shall find me rowing against the stream. I care not who knows it – I write for the general amusement.

Fortunes of Nigel, Introductory Epistle

To confess to you the truth, the works and passages in which I have succeeded have uniformly been written with the greatest rapidity.

Ibid.

I love to have the press thumping, clattering and banging in my rear – it creates the necessity which almost always makes me work best.

Journal, 90

The misfortune of writing fast is that one cannot at the same time write concisely. *Ibid.*, 553

I am but too conscious of having considered the plot only as what Bayes calls the means of bringing in fine things. *Ibid.*, 215

I write grammar as I speak, to make my meaning known, and a solecism in point of composition like a Scotch word in speaking is indifferent to me.

Ibid., 134

A thing may already be so well told in history that Romance ought not in prudence to meddle with it.

Ibid., 503

Where historical characters are introduced it ought only to be incidentally and in such a manner as not to interfere with established truth.

Letters, III.234

After all works of fiction, viz. Cursed Lies, are easier to write and much more popular than the best truths.

Journal, 333

Now this may seem strange but it is quite true, and it is no less so that I have generally written to the middle of one of these novels without having the least idea how it was to end, in short in the *Der donde diere* or hab nab at a venture style of compositions.

Ibid., 433

If I wrote every-day-manners who would read them?
Letters, IV.166

The Big Bow wow strain I can do myself like any now going but the exquisite touch which renders ordinary common-place things and characters interesting from the truth of the description and the sentiment is denied to me.   *Journal,* 114

The women do this better – Edgeworth, Ferrier, Austen have all had their portraits of real society far superior to anything Man vain Man has produced of the like nature.
Ibid., 121

A third rogue writes to tell me ... that he approves of the first three volumes of the *H. of Midlothian* but totally condemns the fourth ... However an author should be reasonably well pleased when three fourths of his works are acceptable to the reader.   *Ibid.,* 32

I am very fond of the Stage which is the only public amusement that I ever indulge in.   *Letters,* III.54

After all as times go the applause of a London audience is so little to be desired that it has always appeared to me that writing for the stage is a most desperate business.   *Ibid.,* IV.473

Avowedly, I will never write for the stage.
Ibid., V.135

Making any serious theatrical attempt is as much out of my mind as flying in a balloon.   *Ibid.,* V.193

To write for low, ill-informed, and conceited actors, whom you must please, for your success is necessarily at their mercy, I cannot away with ... Besides, if this objection were out of the way, I do not think the character of the audience in London is such that one could have the least pleasure in pleasing them.
Ibid., V.339

The unities of time and place have always appeared to
me fopperies, as far as they require close observance of
the French rules. Still, the nearer you can come to them,
it is always, no doubt, the better, because your action
will be more probable. But the unity of action – I mean
that continuity which unites every scene with the other,
and makes the catastrophe the natural and probable
result of all that has gone before – seems to me a critical
rule which cannot safely be dispensed with.

Ibid., VII.146

I am persuaded both children and the lower class of
readers hate books which are written *down* to their
capacity and love those that are more composed for their
elders and betters.

Journal, 308-9

I do not at all like the task of reviewing and have seldom
myself undertaken it – in poetry never – because I am
sensible there is a greater difference of tastes in that
department than in any other and that there is much
excellent poetry which I am not now-a-days able to read
without falling asleep.

Letters, I.398

In general I think it ungentlemanly to wound any
person's feelings through an anonymous publication
unless where conceit or false doctrine strongly calls for
reprobation.

Ibid., XII.243-4

I have refrained as much as human frailty will permit
from all satirical composition.

Journal, 236

Writing to one's friends is the next thing to seeing them.

Letters, I.10

I detest letter writing and envy the Old Hermit of
Prague who never saw pen or ink.

Journal, 78

Scott on Himself

They are funny people the Americans: I saw a paper in which they said my father was a tailor. If he had been an *honest tailor*, I should not have been ashamed of the circumstance; but he was what may be thought as great a phenomenon, for he was an *honest lawyer*, a cadet of a good family, whose predecessors only dealt in pinking and slashing doublets, not in making them.

Letters, VIII.166

From the earliest period of my existence, ballads and other romantic poems I have read or heard as a favourite, and sometimes as an exclusive gratification.

Ibid., I.4

My education was of a very desultory nature not from want of the kindest paternal care but, partly from bad health in early youth, partly from the interruptions seclusions and indulgences, I was too much permitted to study what I liked and when I liked, which was very little and very seldom. To mend the matter I stuffed my brains with all such reading as was never read and in the department of my memory where should be a Roman Patera lo! there is a witches' cauldron. I am more apt to pray to Thor or Woden than Jupiter, think of the fairies oftener than the Dryads and of Bannockburn and Flodden more than Marathon and Pharsalia.

Ibid., II.322-3

I was always a willing listener to tales of broil and battle and hubbub of every kind and now I look back on it I think what a godsend I must have been while a boy to the old Trojans of 1745 nay 1715 who used to frequent my father's house and who knew as little as I did for what market I was laying up the raw materials of their oft told tales.

Ibid., X.238

Any success I may have had in hitting off the Stuarts is, I am afraid, owing to a little old Jacobite leaven which I sucked in with the numerous traditionary tales that amused my infancy.

Ibid., III.140

I became a valiant Jacobite at the age of ten years old; and, even since reason and reading came to my assistance, I have never quite got rid of the impression which the gallantry of Prince Charles made on my imagination.

Ibid., I.343

Like an old fool I must needs remember that I was once the best climber in the High School and had even scaled the castle rock by the precarious path called the *kittle* (*i.e.* ticklish) *nine steps.*

Ibid., IX.266

I myself detested the profession of the bar to which I was bred up.   *Ibid.*, IV.139

My supposed poetical turn ruined me in my profession.

Ibid., I.390

I have a natural love for a soldier which would have been the mode of life I would have chosen in preference to all others but for my lameness.

Ibid., III.351

But if Boney and his invincibles did not come to share the fate of
   'Alexander, king of Macedon,
   Who conquered all the world but Scotland alone',
why, it was not my fault; we dreamed of him, looked for him, and, by our Lady, hoped for him.

Ibid., X.241

Few men, leading a quiet life and without any strong or highly varied change of circumstances, have seen more variety of Society than I – few have enjoyed it more or been *bored*, as it is called, less by the company of tiresome people. I have rarely if ever found anyone out of whom I could not extract amusement or edification.

Journal, 49-50

I generally affect good spirits in company of my family whether I am enjoying them or not. It is too severe to sadden the harmless mirth of others by suffering your own causeless melancholy to be seen. And this species of exertion is, like virtue, its own reward; for the good spirits which are at first simulated become at length real.

Ibid., 354

I have had all my life a longing to do some thing else when I am called to particular labour – a vile contradictory humour which I cannot get rid of.

Ibid., 619

Though I always wonder why it should be so I feel a dislike to order and to task work of all kinds ... what I mean is a detestation of precise order in petty matters – in reading or answering letters, in keeping my papers arranged and in order and so on.

Ibid., 264

I have endeavoured with some success never to trouble myself about fashionable applause or censure or parodies or commendatory verses or being praised in one review or blamed in another.

Letters, IV.29

No man that ever wrote a line despised the *pap* of *praise* so heartily as I do.

Journal, 198

I ... make it a rule never to read the attacks made upon me.

Letters, IV.38

If there be any great advantage in literary fame I have
had it and I certainly do not care at losing it. They cannot
say but what I *had* the *crown*.

Journal, 393

[After the financial crash:] But I will involve no friend
either rich or poor – My own right hand shall do it.

Ibid., 65

In prosperous times I have sometimes felt my fancy and
powers of language flag – but adversity is to me at least
a tonic and bracer. *Ibid.,* 65

Those who do not work from necessity take violent
labour from choice and were necessity out [of] the
question I would take the same sort of literary labour
from choice. *Ibid.,* 555

I … have arrived at a flocci-pauci-nihili-pili-fication of
money and I thank Shenstone for inventing that long
word. *Ibid.,* 107

[On being gazetted Baronet:] Remember I anticipate the
jest 'I like not such *grinning* honour as Sir Walter hath'.

Letters, V.261

I used to be fond of war when I was a younger man, and
longed heartily to be a soldier ; but now I think there is
no prayer in the service with which I could close more
earnestly, than 'Send peace in our time, good Lord'.

Ibid., III.462

The greatest advance of age which I have yet found is
liking a *cat* an animal I detested and becoming fond of a
garden an art which I despised.

Ibid., VII.99

[On his deathbed, to Lockhart:] Be a good man – be
virtuous – be religious – be a good man. Nothing else
will give you any comfort when you come to lie here.

Life, X.217-18

Rules for Living

In literature as in love courage is half the battle.

Journal, 206

It is clear to me that what is least forgiven in a man of any mark or likelihood is want of that article blackguardly called *pluck.* All the fine qualities of genius cannot make amends for it.

Ibid., 347

The great art of life, so far as I have been able to observe, consists in fortitude and perseverance.

Letters, IV.362

Exertion, like virtue, is its own reward.

Waverley, ch. 43

To enjoy leisure, it is absolutely necessary it should be preceded by occupation.

Monastery, Introductory Epistle

After all these interruptions are not such bad things – they make a man keen of the work which he is with-held from … – you stick to it for contradiction's sake.

Journal, 197

No whetter of genius is necessity though said to be the mother of invention.

Ibid., 608

No good man can ever be happy when he is unfit for the career of simple and commonplace duty, and I need not add how many melancholy instances there are of extravagance and profligacy being resorted to, under the pretence of contempt for the common rules of life.

Letters, II.278

Men of genius are not only equally fit but much fitter for the business of the world than dunces, providing always they will give their talents fair play by curbing them with application.

Ibid., III.148

Good advice is easily followed when it jumps with our own sentiments and inclinations.

Ibid., III.346

Life is too short for the indulgence of animosity.

Ibid., II.372

I never have yet found ... that ill-will dies in debt or what is called gratitude distresses herself by frequent payments.

Journal, 102

Enough ill nature to keep your good nature from being abused is no bad ingredient in their disposition who have favours to bestow.

Ibid., 189

To live in bad society will deprave the best manners and to live in good will improve the worst.

Letters, V.496

There is usually an obstinacy in weakness.

Journal, 130

A man of eminence in any line, and perhaps a man of great literary eminence especially, is exposed to a thousand eyes which men, not so celebrated, are safe from – and in consequence, right conduct is much more essential to his happiness than to those who are less watched.

Life, VII.324

Never to be doing nothing.

Ibid., VIII.62

Twist ye, twine ye! even so
Mingle shades of joy and woe,
Hope and fear, and peace and strife,
In the thread of human life.

Guy Mannering, ch. 4

I shall do my duty however. Do what is right come what
will.

Journal, 617

Look not thou on beauty's charming, –
Sit thou still when kings are arming, –
Taste not when the wine-cup glistens, –
Speak not when the people listens, –
Stop thine ear against the singer, –
From the red gold keep thy finger; –
Vacant heart and hand, and eye, –
Easy live and quiet die.

Bride of Lammermoor, ch. 3

Observations & Opinions

Antiquarianism

I do not know any thing which relieves the mind so much from the sullens as trifling discussions about *antiquarian old-womanries* – It is like knitting a stocking, diverting the mind without occupying it.　　*Journal*, 441

Babies

Mrs. Hughes thinks the infant a beauty – Johnie opines that it is not *very* pretty, and Grandpapa supposes it like other newborn children which are as like as a basket of oranges.　　*Ibid.*, 411

I care not for children till they care a little for me.
Ibid., 456

Begging

I never yield to this importunity, thinking it wrong that what I can spare to meritorious poverty of which I hear and see too much should be diverted by impudent importunity.　　*Ibid.*, 504

Bores

Of all the boring machines ever devised your regular and determined story-teller is the most peremptory and powerful in his operations.　　*Letters*, V.211

An efficient bore must always have something respectable about him otherwise no one would permit him to exercise his occupation and bestow his tediousness upon him. – He must be for example a very rich man (which perhaps gives the greatest privilege of all) – or he must be a man of rank and condition too important to be treated sans ceremonie – or a man of learning (often a dreadful bore) or of talents undoubted and privileged – or of pretensions to wisdom and experience – or a great traveller – In short he must have some tangible privilege to exercize his profession. Without something of this kind one would treat a bore as you do a vagrant mendicant and send him off to the workhouse if he presumed to annoy you.   *Ibid., IX.40-1*

Chess

Surely chess-playing is a sad waste of brains.   *Life, I.174*

Committees

I have no turn for these committees and yet I get always jammed into them. They take up a cruel deal of time in a way very unsatisfactory.   *Journal, 562*

Many men care less to gain their point than they do to play the orator and be listened to for a certain time.
Ibid., 415

An orator is like a top: let him alone and he must stop one time or another. Flog him and he may go on for ever.
Ibid., 382

Common people

The common people, the severest critics of the conduct of their betters.   *Ivanhoe, ch. 2*

How willing the vulgar are to gull themselves when they can find no one else to take the trouble.
Journal, 47

Consolation

O! many a shaft, at random sent,
Finds mark the archer little meant!
And many a word, at random spoken,
May soothe or wound a heart that's broken!
Lord of the Isles, canto 5

Deceit

O what a tangled web we weave,
When first we practise to deceive!

Marmion, canto 6

Dentists

He that has rid a man of the tooth-ache is well entitled to
command a part of his time.

Journal, 198

Doctors

No disparagement to the Esculapian art, they are bad
guessers.

Letters, VIII.257

Drinking

A glass of good wine is a gracious creature and
reconciles poor mortality to itself, and that is what few
things can do.

Journal, 253

Without being a veteran Vice, a Grey Iniquity, like
Falstaff, I think an occasional jolly bout if not carried to
excess improved society. Men were put into good
humour 'when the good wine did its good office'; the
jest, the song, the speech had double effect; men were
happy for the night and better friends ever after because
they had been so.

Ibid., 141

Wine unveils the passions and throws away restraint but
it does not create habits or opinions which did not
previously exist in the mind.

Letters, VI.438

Depend upon it, of all vices drinking is the most
incompatible with greatness.

Life, I.200

Farewells

I hate red eyes and blowing of noses.

Journal, 25

Favourites

Although a favourite, as the poet assures us, has no friend, he seldom fails to have both followers and flatterers.
Fortunes of Nigel, ch. 16

Field sports

In every point of view field-sports are preferable to the in-doors amusement of a Billiard table, which is too often the lounging place for idle young officers where there is nothing to be got but a habit of throwing away time and an acquaintance with the very worst society.
Letters, V.482

Forgiveness

The mass of mankind will respect a monarch stained with actual guilt, more than one whose foibles render him only ridiculous.
Fortunes of Nigel, ch. 27

Ghosts

Ghosts are only seen where they are believed.
Letters, X.372

Laughter

Real laughter is a thing as rare as real tears.
Journal, 286

Good humour can spread a certain inexpressible charm over the plainest human countenance.
Black Dwarf, ch. 6

Newspapers

The Newspapers told about fifty lies about this matter as usual but one would have little to do who should mind them.
Letters, III.404-5

Nothing but a thorough-going Blackguard ought to attempt the daily press.
Journal, 542

Phrenology

There is a certain kind of cleverish men either
half-educated or cock-brained by nature who are
attached to that same turnipology.   *Ibid.,* 257

Preservation

Am clear in my own mind a ruin should be protected
but never repaired.   *Ibid.,* 579

Proverbial sayings

Better a finger off, as ay wagging.   *Redgauntlet,* ch. 2

It's ill speaking between a fou man and a fasting.
                                          Ibid., Letter 11

It's ill taking the breeks aff a wild Highlandman.
                                       Fortunes of Nigel, ch. 5

My foot is on my native heath.
                                              Rob Roy, ch. 34

The ae half of the warld thinks the tither daft.
                                          Redgauntlet, ch. 7

There's a gude time coming.
                                              Rob Roy, ch. 32

Rain

Here is a vile day, downright rain, which ... of course
annihilates a part of the stock of human happiness. But
what says the proverb of your true rainy day?
   Tis good for book, tis good for work
   For cup and can or knife and fork.

                                              Journal, 298

Removals

A removal, or what we call a *flitting* ... of all bores under
the cope of heaven, is bore the most tremendous.
                                              Letters, I.224

Servants

Servants are fond of the woeful: it gives such
consequence to the person who communicates bad news.

Journal, 137

Tipping

I own I like to pay postilions and waiters rather more
liberally than perhaps is right. I hate grumbling and sour
faces and the whole saving will not exceed a guinea or
two for being cursed and damned from Dan to
Beersheba.   *Ibid.*, 456

Trees

Jock, when ye hae naething else to do, ye may be ay
sticking in a tree; it will be growing, Jock, when ye're
sleeping.   *Heart of Mid-Lothian*, ch. 8

Planting and pruning trees I could work at from
morning till night and if my poetical revenues enable me
to have a few acres of my own that is one of the
principal pleasures I look forward to. There is too a sort
of self-congratulation, a little tickling self-flattery in the
idea that while you are pleasing and amusing yourself
you are really seriously contributing to the future
welfare of the country and that your very acorn may
send its ribs of oak to future victories like Trafalgar.

Letters, II.402-3

Valets

Although a man cannot be a hero to his valet, his valet in
sickness becomes of great use to him.

Journal, 49

*

To all, to each, a fair good-night,
And pleasing dreams, and slumbers light!

Marmion, L'envoy